THE POWER IN
LETTING GO

THE POWER IN
LETTING GO

CALVIN MILLER

TYNDALE HOUSE PUBLISHERS, INC.
WHEATON, ILLINOIS

Visit Tyndale's exciting Web site at www.tyndale.com

Designed by Jenny Swanson

Edited by Jeremy P. Taylor

Published in association with the literary agency of Alive Communications, Inc., 7680 Goddard Street, Suite 200, Colorado Springs, CO 80920.

ISBN 0-8423-6177-4

Printed in the United States of America

07 06 05 04 03
5   4   3   2   1

CONTENTS

✳ ✳ ✳ ✳

PREFACE

It has been almost a century since the *Titanic* surrendered to the icy North Atlantic. The arctic waters strangled hundreds of souls with the icy fingers of paralysis. Some found themselves clinging to the debris of the disaster. Those who threw them ring buoys and ropes called out, "Let go—and take hold! Let go of the trash, take hold of rings and rescue ropes." Those who heard the cry had no more than four minutes to obey. The cold and killing waters of the North Atlantic allowed them only 240 seconds of life. From freezing to survival was a brief trip. Letting go to live is often a hurried choice of courage.

In a similar way, the titanic blessings of God are never available for long. Life is short. We must number our days (Psalm 90:12, KJV) in hurried minutes. We must prioritize in seconds. We must let go of our grasp on temporary trash to take hold of things eternal.

We must relinquish and rely.

We must let go and take hold.

This is the simple recipe by which God rescues us from small-time living to teach us the glories of yielded greatness.

My life is in bondage to an old cliché: "All I will hold in my cold dead hand is what I have given away." It is a saying akin to those haunting words of the Savior, "Whoever clings to this life will lose it, and whoever loses this life will save it" (Luke 17:33). All in all, I'm convinced I can never take hold of anything that matters till I have let go of everything that doesn't. But I am not naive. I've been infected with consumerism. I've developed a chronic case of "I've gotta' have it." My greed all too often overcomes my self-denial. I hang on to things that are worthless, and therefore I lose my grip on things of value. I forever hear my Lord say, "How can you and I ever walk hand in hand when your hands are so full of such poor, temporary treasures?"

I served for years as a pastor, and I have seen some regrettable results of groveling for influence. I have seen church workers competing with each other by grasping after corporate power. I knew one pastor who measured his whole self-worth in terms of his competition with fellow ministers in a race to build the biggest church in town. He had almost maneuvered himself into a position to win when his elders fired him. I then watched him try, painfully, to formulate a new self-worth when his plot to be super-pastor was taken from him. Sadly, he has never recovered.

The closer I draw to Christ, the more I understand that any type of power that can be seized usually hurts others. I have rarely seen anything beautiful come from those who pursue power. But what I *have* seen is that even the worst corporate Caesar, when he finally unclenches his grasping fists, can reach freely for significance. One of my best friends became real only when the company of which he had long been CEO gave him his "gold watch" on a coffee break and then told him to

clean out his desk. When his desolation
ended, he found reasons to live that were far
better than those furnished to him by the
corporate ladder. With Christ at the helm, my
friend came to a better understanding of his
own significance.

We have the Savior for our role model.
Jesus did not clutch after the competitive life.
He did the opposite—he gave up his life! "No
one can take my life from me," he said, "I lay
down my life voluntarily" (John 10:18). Jesus
released his grasp on the one thing most of us
treasure most—life itself—and in his empty
hand his Father placed the prize of world
redemption. Christ could only take hold of our
lives by releasing the hold he had on his own.

"Let go and take hold," the angels shout to
all who adore Christ.

"Let go and take hold," they shouted to a
priest named Damien, who gave up his health
in order to minister to lepers on Hawaii's
dreaded Molokai Island.

"Let go and take hold," they shouted to a cobbler named William Carey, who left his shop in England and devoted himself to translation work in India that led to copies of the Bible in forty Indian languages.

"Let go and take hold," they shouted to a nun called Teresa, who gave up Albania and gained Calcutta.

"Let go and take hold," they shouted to Jim Elliott, a Wheaton College graduate who gave up his life in Ecuador to seize the martyr's gate of splendor.

"Let go and take hold!" is God's call to you.

To what are you now clinging? What can you release so that God might fill your grasp with heaven's treasures?

I have a friend only slightly older than me, who had dreams of becoming a great pianist. Her dreams were heady, and she drove herself to own them. She practiced the piano day and night. She went to church sometimes, but her

CALVIN MILLER

dreams of glory made no real place for God.
Her life was crammed with her own goals.

Then polio came, a crippling paralysis that
no one seemed to understand. This monstrous
disease feeds on young bodies and eats at
bone, nerve, and sinew till it kills. Thankfully,
polio is now an all but forgotten disease, but
during the 1940s and 1950s, polio made para-
plegics of thousands of children.

My friend was a teenager, and the God
that she long ignored suddenly became her
obsession. "God," she cried, "leave my hands
whole, and give me one good leg for the
sustain pedal, and I will use my music only for
you."

She relinquished her all consuming, selfish
dreams . . . and God moved. Her disease
destroyed her left leg. She wore a brace on it
for the rest of her life. But her right leg and
both her hands became God's instruments.
Her life became his symphony. Each time I
heard her play, I understood anew the power

of letting go. What she gave up was but little. What she took hold of was all-significant.

She confided to me how grateful she was that God had allowed her to contract polio. The contagion had birthed in her the power to let go of everything that didn't matter to take hold of everything that did.

Another friend of mine played minor league baseball in the Dodgers organization. I don't really know if he was good enough to play for the major leagues. Sometimes I teased him that he was destined to end his career "20,000 leagues beneath the majors." But he was successful where he was. Nonetheless, after he became a Christian, he abandoned his athletic career. Then he traveled around the country giving his testimony as an ex-athlete. Wherever he spoke he threw his baseball glove into the audience and said, "This is what I gave up for Jesus."

The drama of all he had given up caused me to despise my poor testimony. I was a

CALVIN MILLER

wimp who had nothing of value to give up.
My testimony produced nothing! No crowd,
no admiration, no love offering! In coming to
faith I had merely gone from being a secular
wimp to being a Christian wimp. My becoming a Christian was not a grand moment for
God, only for me.

But in time I realized the fault in such
thoughts. In reality, what my baseball-player
friend had relinquished and what I had relinquished were both of small consequence.
Although it seemed to me that he had given
up far more, what has anyone given up that
really matters in comparison to taking on
Christ? We have all let go of nothing so that
we might gain something.

Still, we tend to cherish things that have
no value. Why don't we let go? I can't say for
sure. But I suspect that the greatest weapon in
Satan's arsenal is the trick of teaching us to
cherish nothingness—and most people buy
into his lies. Most die clinging to nothing.

It is the worst of folly.

    It is the weakest way to live.

It would be better

    To relinquish our appetites and find

        God's hidden manna:

To let go of all things—

    Our clutching after air,

To leave our grasping habits

    And find the Savior there.

✻ ✻ ✻ ✻

MOSES
OF STICKS AND
COBRAS

Moses: the man who spoke sternly and carried a big stick! When he raised his ironwood shepherd's staff, the world fled before him. He seems to have carried it with him everywhere. With it he herded the sheep of his father-in-law, Jethro. With it he divided the seas and stabbed the rock with watery wounds.

Where did he get this old rod? Who knows for sure? Perhaps he had retrieved it from the storm-worn heights of Sinai. Perhaps his steely stick had been forged by the gales of the Midian desert. Wherever he got it, the wood of Moses' staff must have been twisted and broken and healed beneath its splintery bark a thousand times, until the fibers of its heart were scarred beyond bending. Oh, it was strong! Moses held on to it, leaned on it, and flagged it in the devils face. He used it to bludgeon trouble from his path. I imagine that in some ways it symbolized to Moses the strength of Jehovah himself.

Moses had his rod with him on the day he went into the wilderness near Sinai, before he became Israel's deliverer. There where the bush burned, God wanted to have a talk with Moses (see Exodus 4:1-5).

"What do you have there in your hand?" God asked.

"A shepherd's staff."

"Throw it on the ground," God said. *Let go of your precious stick!*

Moses wondered at God's words, but he opened his hand, and gravity instantly sucked the staff flat to the ground.

Then, to his amazement, the rod became a cobra!

A cobra? Can we know this? No. But I think God's power transcends the pettiness of garter snakes. Cobras were common snakes in Sinai, and this snake must have been at least as dangerous as a cobra, for we're told that "Moses was terrified, so he turned and ran away" (Exodus 4:3).

Cobra or not, the snake coiled and hissed at Moses. Its pink lightning tongue forked forth fear. It poised for a fanged showdown, and Moses fled before it.

Could God not have changed his stick to a cobra as he held it? Wouldn't that have been even more terrifying? Perhaps. But God demanded relinquishment. We must let go of things to define them. Only as we release the puzzling things in life can we get far enough away from them to gain enough perspective to understand them.

> GOD HAS TREASURES HE WANTS TO GIVE US, BUT FIRST WE MUST LAY DOWN OUR SYMBOLS OF SELF-CONFIDENCE.

This drama of the cudgel and the cobra was as short as it was fiery. One act, one scene, one relinquishment! Then the curtain fell. At God's command, Moses took hold of the snake by its tail, and it became a staff again.

But I've always wondered whether Moses didn't ever afterward regard his staff with special awe. Did he keep his eye on his unpredictable rod? Did he take care never to lay it too close to his bed at night . . . just in case? Did he refuse to set it on the ground too near his knee when he knelt to have a drink? I'll bet he never forgot on which end of the staff the head had appeared, just in case it was suddenly more than he wanted it to be.

God has treasures he wants to give us, but first we must lay down our symbols of self-confidence. We must not be afraid to face our weakness. When we do, we find that we are not so weak as we thought! Most people never see their potential, for they are too shackled to their staffs of security to trust God in the fearsome art of snake making. So the power they might own is confined to the rock-hard security they will not release from their stingy grasp.

Letting go is God's plan to change the world. This principle stands at the very center of Scripture. Again and again we see that God is in the business of using people who have learned the power of relinquishment:

Abraham let go of his homeland, and a nation was born.

Hannah let go of her child, and a prophet was born.

Joseph let go of hostility toward his treacherous brothers, and his own sons shared in the inheritance of Canaan.

Elisha let go of his plow and became the conscience of Israel.

Naaman let go of his self-image, and his leprosy was cleansed.

Peter let go of his net and seined men for the kingdom.

Barnabas let go of his field on Cyprus and became better known than Nero.

Paul surrendered his hatred of Christians and reached a continent for Christ.

Letting go is also our key to power. Relinquishment is the path to spiritual riches. The surrender of our insignificance is the key to real significance.

So this book is a call—a call to take the sticks of our pride and throw them down.

Our days of foolish weakness will then be ended.

The awesome and terrible power of God flies to those wise enough to let go.

Littleness is past.

A bright serpent waits to jump from our drab, grasping contentment.

We are mightier than we know!

We have only to let go of death and take hold of life!

Let go and take hold!

✳ ✳ ✳ ✳

INTRODUCTION

✹ ✹ ✹ ✹

Whatever this world might give: status, success, glamour, wealth, or pleasure, God offers something far greater—an inheritance that is imperishable and undefiled and will not fade away (1 Peter 1:4). Moses gave up his lofty role as Pharaoh's son because he was looking to his reward (Hebrews 11:26). The early Christians joyfully relinquished their homes and all that they owned, for they knew they had a better and lasting possession awaiting them (Hebrews 10:34). God has blessed us with an incredible life on this earth, but he did not intend that it should capture our affections.

—TRICIA MCCARY RHODES[1]

✹ ✹ ✹ ✹

TRAPEZE THEORY

I have tried throughout my life to operate by the "trapeze theory" when making career decisions. I don't let go of the swing in my right hand until I've grasped the second bar firmly with my left. Why? Because letting go is fearsome work. By not letting go of one job until I'm convinced that the next one won't fall through, I gain a sense of security. But let's face it—while my methods might work well for job security, they would make a horrible trapeze act! The appearance of flying would be swallowed up in leaden clumsiness. All trapeze artists know you must let go—even at terrifying heights—if you want to soar.

For years I have taught seminary students, attempting to show them the way to better communication. Many times I have watched them lose the force of their calling by telling God exactly how or where they would prefer to serve. I had one student who loved the South and made it clear to God that once he was out of school he would minister only in Alabama. I tried to no avail to tell him that before God would use him anywhere, he would have to hand God a world atlas and say, "I'll go wherever you want me, Lord."

In 1845, a British explorer named John Franklin led an expedition to search for the Northwest Passage. When their ships became icebound, they set out across the ice on foot. They never returned home. Years later, their ice-preserved corpses were found lying among stores of fine wine, bone china, and crystal goblets. The explorers had not been able to let go of their love of the good life. They would have been wiser to carry less china and more blankets.

Langdon Gilkey was an English teacher at a university in Japanese-occupied China at the start of Word War II. He, along with many other American civilians in China, was interned in a concentration camp during the war. Gilkey later wrote that many of his fellow prisoners tried to carry with them into their imprisonment their jewels, mantle-clocks, and carts of bulky treasures. They found it hard to let go of the good life. Later, prison life taught them how to barter gilded clocks for real necessities like eggs and onions.

In church we often sing hymns like "Wherever he leads, I'll go" or "Take my life and let it be consecrated, Lord, to thee." The clear message of these songs is: "I've let go of my sacred geography. I've relinquished all my claims to my own career dreams. Do with me what you will, God." Yet so often we fail to demonstrate the relinquishment of which we sing. We refuse to let go of one trapeze before soaring on to the next. We love our dead sticks too much to let them go, and we fail to discover the wonderful terror of cobra making.

DINING LIKE A KING

The joys that come from letting go never end with the relinquisher. Others, too, are blessed by the surrender.

I have eaten in the finest of restaurants throughout many countries. But the most memorable meal of my life was one I ate with a poor couple in Latin America who invited me to dinner. When I arrived at their home, we dined on dry toast and scrambled eggs. We had vanilla wafers for dessert. Still the laughter flowed like expensive wine. How had this poor-but-wealthy couple ever come to delight in such simplicity? I think they had learned how to change sticks to cobras. Though the world might scorn their hard-bought wealth, I knew they had been made rich by the art of letting go. They had let go of their romance with materialism, and God had provided them richer fare. As a result, their meager table had become too royal for apologies.

> IF WE LOVE OUR DEAD STICKS TOO MUCH TO LET THEM GO, WE WILL FAIL TO DISCOVER THE WONDERFUL TERROR OF COBRA MAKING.

Another equally poor couple I met took me out to dinner at a Pizza Hut in San Jose, Costa Rica. It was only pizza, yet it seemed as if we were seated at the marriage supper of the Lamb. Pepperoni? No. Ours was richer fare eaten from plates of gold. Then when I went to the cashier's stand and tried to pay, the cashier told me that my host had already taken care of the bill. When I protested, the missionary told me readily, "God instructed me to bless you." Blessing indeed! He and his wife had let go of what was for them a significant sum to buy dinner, and I shared with them the blessing of their relinquishment.

So here's to our anthem of spiritual liberty, our hymn of Christian possibility:

Let go, and let God have his wonderful
    way,
Your darkness will vanish, your night turn
        to day.
Let go and let God have his way.

THE RELINQUISHMENT TO-DO LIST

There are four major areas of letting go. As you attempt to master this quartet of princi-ples, you will discover the truth of D.L. Moody's famous comment, "The world has yet to discover the man who is fully committed to God." Becoming fully committed is a discipline of years. Relinquishment is a life-long process. No one can master it all at once.

> THE JOYS THAT COME FROM LETTING GO DON'T STOP WITH THE RELINQUISHER. OTHERS CAN BE BLESSED ALONG WITH YOU.

Here is your let-go list. As you begin to release these four things, you will begin to take hold of the image of Christ.

First, we must release our desire for the material world.

Wait! Don't throw this book down!

I know of no greater challenge than letting

go of the material. Materialism is a universal affliction. I wish I could say that only the super wealthy offend God by loving their possessions too much. But those who have less money often cherish their little as much as the wealthy cherish their plenty.

We usually hoard material things because we believe they are a kind of security. Hard times seem cruel and threaten to dispossess us. But the more we cherish our goods in the face of difficulty, the less we own them—and the more they own us. No matter how much we have, we never believe we have enough! Even multi-millionaires, when asked what it would take to make them truly happy, often reply, "Just a little more."

Jesus told a story about a foolish rich man who was convinced that the answer to his insecurities was bigger barns:

> *A rich man had a fertile farm that produced fine crops. In fact, his barns were full to*

*overflowing. So he said, "I know! I'll tear
down my barns and build bigger ones. Then
I'll have room enough to store everything.
And I'll sit back and say to myself, My
friend, you have enough stored away for
years to come. Now take it easy! Eat, drink,
and be merry!" (Luke 12:16-19)*

The man in this parable solved his problem the same way we so often do—he hung on to the stuff he counted as his salvation. But the end of the story indicates that he would have done much better to let go. The man died, and all his planning was for nothing. The message is crystal clear: "A person is a fool to store up earthly wealth but not have a rich relationship with God" (Luke 12:21). Letting go is the only way to keep what is truly important.

Most of us want to appear as charitable as Mother Teresa while we act like Ebenezer Scrooge. Jesus ever stands in the wings waiting for us to abdicate our folly. The late Jim Elliott expressed this truth eloquently: "He is no fool who gives what he cannot keep to gain what he cannot lose."

Second, we must let go of our time.

Time is the great nonrenewable commodity. It moves constantly past us, and once past, it is gone forever. God starts the wind-down clock of our lives even before the umbilical cord has been snipped, and the ticking doesn't pause so much as a millisecond until our life is over. I am now sixty-six, and on lonely midnights when the house is still, it seems to me I can hear the grating of sand on silicate—the rush of granular time through the neck of the hourglass.

I try to live by three passages of Scripture. My Old Testament passage is:

"Teach us to make the most of our time,
so that we may grow in wisdom."
(Psalm 90:12)

The first of my two New Testament passages is:

> *"Be careful how you live, not as fools but as those who are wise. Make the most of every opportunity for doing good in these evil days."* (Ephesians 5:15-16)

Making the most of every opportunity for doing good is the process of taking the seconds and decades I would have lavished on myself, and depositing those seconds—as if they were money—in God's bank account. For indeed our hours are expendable currency. The King James Version calls this process "redeeming the time." All that will matter when we run out of time is the time we have given to God.

The second of my New Testament passages reads:

> *"How do you know what will happen tomorrow? For your life is like the morning*

fog—it's here a little while, then it's gone."
(James 4:14)

The clock outruns us all. Hoarding the hours
only tells the world we unsuccessfully compete
with the spinning sweep of the second hand.
God is waiting for us to say, "Lord, here's my
watch and calendar. I want to serve you full-
time and never watch the clock."

I am directed by the words of a little
needlepoint I once saw on an old woman's
wall:

"Only one life, t'will soon be past
Only what's done for Christ will last."

Third, we must let go of our dreams.
One of the happiest physicians I have ever
known practices medicine in rural Mexico.
One of the most miserable physicians I've met
has a half-million-dollar practice in America.
The happiness or misery of these two very

en centers around each one's willingness to let go of his career dreams. Both of
them, as young men,
dreamed of being
doctors. Both dreamed
of receiving the social
and material bonuses
that would be part of a
future in medicine. But
one hoarded and cher-
ished his dreams. The
other gave them to
God for renovation.

> MOST OF US
> WANT TO APPEAR
> AS CHARITABLE
> AS MOTHER
> TERESA WHILE
> WE ACT LIKE
> EBENEZER
> SCROOGE.

Guess which is the happy one today!

There is an old poem that offers us this
logic:

> I had built my castles and reared them
> high
> Till their steeples pierced the blue of
> the sky.
> I had sworn to rule with an iron mace,

When I met the Master, face to face.
And then I fell at his feet that day
  While my castles melted and vanished
    away.
My thoughts are now for the souls of men,
  I've lost my life to find it again.
Since that day in a quiet place,
  When I met the Master face to face."[2]

To relinquish our dreams is to take hold of the
will of God.

Fourth, we must let go of our image.

Oh, how we fight to appear to be successful
achievers. We want our friends to believe it,
and even more, we want to believe it
ourselves. Our self-image and the way we
appear to others are perhaps the most difficult
of all things for us to surrender. Even when
we give our lives and everything else to Christ,
we feel we must look good both to ourselves
and to our community of friends.

Sadly, our failure to relinquish our image often leads to hypocrisy. We want to appear "holy," so we hide our sins. We want to appear "sacrificial," so we drive the cheap car to church. We want to appear "loving," so we smile a lot. Soon, "how we don't want to appear" begins to dominate our behavior. We don't want to appear "stingy," so we put our money in the offering plate in large bills, particularly if others are watching. We don't want to appear "selfish" with our time, so we join every organization in the church.

> ALL THAT WILL MATTER WHEN WE RUN OUT OF TIME IS THE TIME WE HAVE GIVEN TO GOD.

In the process of appearing to be godly, we find we are fooling ourselves and others. We develop a kind of "humble pride" in our mock meekness. We don't want real modesty. We want to appear to have it. We don't want real humility; real humility is hard bought. The only

way you can get it is by humiliation, and humiliation usually lies at the end of a season of
shame. Who needs that? We want to look good!

But the fact is that shame for our sins and
true humility in the face of God's greatness are
essential if we desire God's favor. We need to
rid ourselves of our bogus self-image. Though
perhaps odious, humiliation is a necessary
part of life if we desire to live for Christ.

Jesus taught us this in dying naked before
his mother. His humiliation was our redemption, but even better than that, it taught us the
power of genuine modesty of spirit. To be
openly and publicly humiliated divests us of
phony, false images. This is why Paul said in
Galatians 2:19-20, "I have been crucified with
Christ. I myself no longer live, but Christ lives
in me. So I live my life in this earthly body by
trusting in the Son of God, who loved me and
gave himself for me."

Why would Paul intentionally construct a
view of himself as an executed criminal? He

was identifying with Jesus, who on Good Friday could offer no greater image to the world than that of being "numbered with the transgressors" (Mark 15:28, KJV).

> THOUGH PERHAPS ODIOUS, HUMILITY IS A NECESSARY PART OF LIFE IF WE ARE TO LIVE WITH CHRIST.

Paul further wrote in Philippians 3:10, "I can really know Christ and experience the mighty power that raised him from the dead. I can learn what it means to suffer with him, sharing in his death." Paul wanted the shame of Calvary to fall on him so that he would never give himself to the pursuit of an empty reputation.

So may it be for us.

Come! Let us set out together on an odyssey of relinquishment!

Let us attack each of these four areas of holding on to see how we may best let them go.

Let us let go to let God have his way.

Let us surrender our little to own his all.

Let us relinquish our weakness and take
hold of power.

Let us cry out to God,

"Oh God!
We have emptied our pockets for riches
untold.
We have laid our clock on altars of
gold.
We have laid our sour dreams on the
ledges of fear.
We will honor no more how we long
to appear.
We shall strip away pride with its focus
and show.
We will trust you, relinquish, and let
ourselves go."

CHAPTER ONE

✹ ✹ ✹ ✹

LETTING GO
OF THE MATERIAL

✳ ✳ ✳ ✳

The Father was ever showing Thee what he was doing in the unseen and eternal depths. Indeed, it seemed that Thou wert more occupied in beholding the things which were unseen than those which were seen. Thine eye was ever on the dial-plate of eternity, and thine ear attent to the note of the tide on its shore. Thou didst nothing that was not in the pattern shown Thee on the mount of fellowship; but whatever was wrought there Thou didst here. Teach me to live like this.

—F. B. MEYER[1]

✳ ✳ ✳ ✳

ONLY ONE MASTER

Jesus calls us to the singular adoration of himself. We can only be his if we agree not to place our love for him alongside any other passion. Our desire for material things and our love of Christ always rise as combatants forcing us to decide which will have our affection.

A rich young man once came to Jesus and asked, "What good things must I do to have eternal life?" Jesus told him he must keep the commandments. The man replied that he had always kept all the commandments. Jesus told him that he still lacked one thing.

"What is it I lack?" asked the rich young ruler.

"Love me more than you love your money," said Jesus, in effect.

The Bible says that the man left Jesus sadly because he had many possessions (see Matthew 19:16-22).

Why shouldn't we love our material wealth as much as we love Jesus? Because to love anything as much as we love God is to create an idol in our lives. What we love more than God becomes our god.

> TO LOVE ANYTHING ELSE AS MUCH AS WE LOVE JESUS IS ADULTERY OF THE HEART.

To love anything else as much as we love Jesus is adultery of the heart. The lordship of Jesus is a singular affair we cannot share with our desire to have the good stuff of life. Jesus himself said it: "No one can serve two masters. For you will hate one and love the other, or be devoted to one and despise the other. You cannot serve both God and money" (Matthew 6:24).

Christianity is a monotheistic faith. *Monotheism* means "single-God-ism." It means forcing ourselves to remember that heaven owns no double throne. Neither do our hearts. It is simply not possible for Jesus to share his command over us with all our baser passions.

TRUE FREEDOM

One of A.W. Tozer's principles for the deeper life was this: never *have* to own anything. There are good reasons for owning things like a home or a car, but there are no reasons for *having* to own either. When we acknowledge that we do not *need* to own our possessions, we will not cling to them too tightly, and they will never lay claim to our lives. The things that we feel we must have in order to be complete are the things most likely to own us.

Letting go of our felt need for material things is a big step toward freedom from debt. When we don't feel compelled to own something, we enable ourselves to make intelligent decisions about what we're buying and why, rather than selling our souls to impulse purchases and mounting bills. Freedom from debt is a great freedom indeed. The crushing load of credit-card debt is an encumbrance almost universally acquired by those souls who "had to have" something but couldn't wait until they could actually pay for it. So they bought it and put their obligation to pay for it somewhere out in the future. Buy now, pay later.

The "I have to own this right now" urge is the mother of much mischief.

> JESUS CALLS US TO TREASURE ONLY THE INTANGIBLE, FOR ONLY THOSE THINGS WILL WE BE ABLE TO KEEP IN THE END.

INTANGIBLES

I am addicted to the movie *City of Joy*, which is based on a book by Dominique Lapierre. It is the tale of Max Lowe, an American doctor who abandoned his lucrative medical practice and went to Calcutta, India, trying to find peace after losing a child on the operating table. During the course of the story, Lowe becomes involved in helping destitute slum-dwellers by giving them medical care. As he becomes more and more involved in the lives of the people around him, Lowe realizes that only those who have relinquished all things can adequately serve those who own nothing.

Shortly after reading the book upon which this movie is based, I had the opportunity to travel to Calcutta, where I discovered some pagan priests who had learned the principle of relinquishment. Those priests sacrifice goats every day at the temple of the goddess Kali, Calcutta's namesake (*Kali Cutta*, I am told, is Bengali for "City of Kali"). The priests sacrifice goats and mix the meat with rice. Then they serve it on banana leaves to the thronging poor of Calcutta. But what they are really sacrificing is themselves. Witnessing their self-denial, I asked myself, *If I were a starving Indian with no possessions, would I not adore even a pagan priest with a clump of rice on a banana leaf?* While self-sacrifice alone cannot admit us to the presence of God, it is an admirable virtue wherever it is found. Even in the temple of a pagan god, relinquishment causes blessing.

There are many reasons I love Jesus, but chief among them is that he opted to identify with the poor. Jesus renounced his ownership of the planet to give hope to those who would never own anything of material substance.

I love Jesus for dying with nothing but a robe that became the object of gamblers' depraved desires.

> JESUS GAVE UP EVERYTHING, AND HE LOOKS AT US WITH EYES OF SWIMMING ENTREATY, ASKING US TO DO THE SAME.

Jesus calls us to treasure only the intangible, for only those things will we be able to keep in the end. Ultimately, we will have to leave behind all our material possessions. "All we will hold in our cold, dead hand is what we have given away" is truly a cliché of magnificence. "No hearse was ever coupled to a U-Haul trailer" is another. The only things we can take with us are those things we have given to Jesus, never regarding as our own.

REDUCED TO POVERTY

In the film *Brother Sun, Sister Moon,* filmmaker
Franco Zefferelli tells us of a rift that grew
between the young Saint Francis of Assisi and
his father. Francis's father believed that being
wealthy was the most reasonable of life goals.
Francis, however, refused to believe that
riches were the world's great good. His stance
drew the admiration of the destitute, but his
father could not fathom why his son loved the
poor so ardently.

Finally the relationship between father and
son broke down completely. In a public
moment of confrontation, Francis turned his
back on his father's wealth and his own future
inheritance. Then he made the ultimate state-
ment of rejecting all material things: he took
off the costly brocade robe his father had
given him and let it fall to the ground. He
stood there utterly naked. The wealthy of
Assisi cast down their eyes, but Francis lifted
up his head, for he knew that the shame of

standing naked before people was nothing
compared to the sin of being naked before
God with nothing to offer but poor human
wealth. "I am born again," he said, and walked
away wearing nothing.

He who was rich had made himself poor
for the sake of his Savior, with whom he was
deeply in love. And Francis's relinquishment
didn't end there! I have read Ugolino's *Little
Flowers of Saint Francis* many times. It is the
tale of Francis's conversion. If it is true that
Francis kissed lepers, his embrace of these
eroded bodies proves that he counted his very
life to be worth little in comparison with the
value of caring for others.

Francis realized a great truth: Jesus, Lord
of all, came to earth in the form of a mere
man. He who owned all things reduced
himself to poverty to become a man.

Christ's great submission to poverty was
captured by Alphonsus Maria de Liguori,
who wrote:

*Jesus Christ could have saved mankind
without suffering and dying. Yet, in order to
prove to us how much He loved us, He chose
for Himself a life full of tribulations. . . . His
Passion began, not merely a few hours
before His death, but from the first moment
of His birth. He was born in a stable where
everything served to torment Him. His sense
of sight was hurt by seeing nothing but the
rough, black walls of the cave; His sense of
smell was hurt by the stench of the dung
from the beasts in the stable. . . .*

*Shortly after His birth He was forced to
flee into Egypt, where He spent several years
of His childhood in poverty and misery. His
boyhood and early manhood in Nazareth
were passed in hard work and obscurity.
And finally, in Jerusalem, He died on a
cross, exhausted with pain and anguish.*[4]

Saint Alphonsus Maria de Liguori also
wrote of an exchange between Saint Margaret

of Cortona and her counselor priest. When he saw that the woman continually wept, the priest said, "Margaret, stop crying and cease your lamenting, for God has surely forgiven you your offences against Him."

But she replied, "Father, how can I cease to weep, since I know that my sins kept my Lord Jesus in pain and suffering during all His life?"[5]

In a far less elegant mode, in the little Baptist church where I was baptized, we used to sing of Christ:

"Out of the ivory palaces
    Into a world of woe,
Only His great eternal love,
    Made my Savior go."[6]

Jesus is the role model of our relinquishment. He said, "A servant is not greater than the master. Nor are messengers than the one who sends them" (John 13:16). Jesus gave up everything, and he looks at us with eyes of swimming entreaty, asking us to do the same.

We own nothing that may not be surrendered.

Surely our Lord has left us with this song:

"What shall I give thee Master,
Thou who gavest all for me.
Shall I give less of what I possess
Or shall I give all to Thee?"

It is a fair question. Dare we call anything our own when Jesus has given his all?

Yet to relinquish *is* to own; what we gain by letting go will ultimately make us the envy of millionaires.

✳ ✳ ✳ ✳

CHAPTER TWO

SURRENDERING
OUR TIME

✹ ✹ ✹ ✹

Father, I really prefer to rely on myself . . . on
what I can do . . . what I can have. I say that my
self-reliance is a good thing, so I don't put
demands on others. But, in fact, I want my way!
And I don't like being disappointed. Teach me,
Father, how to rest all my demands and
desires in you . . . and to let you transform
them into the desire to be strong in you.
For you alone are eternal.
—THOMAS À KEMPIS[7]

✹ ✹ ✹ ✹

THE TIME THAT REMAINS

The first machine was the clock, said Lewis Mumford. I'm not sure whether he was correct or not. But regardless of whether the clock was the *first* machine, it has become the *dominant* machine of our culture. We are brutalized by pendulums. Neurotic tick-tocks drive the hurried schedules of our lives.

God wants our hours and years, but we are reluctant to give them to him. Why? Do our small, too-secular engagements have that much significance? I imagine myself keeping track of my schedule by wearing a Mickey Mouse watch. Those three-fingered, white-gloved hands sweep the hours and minutes of my Mickey Mouse schedule. When I think of all the times I have struggled against God's call to surrender my time, it is as if I am telling God not to bother me—the appointments I measure in Mickey Mouse minutes are more important than his divine desires.

I have a great friend who, fifteen years ago,

at the age of fifty, recommitted his life to Christ. But a darkness inhabited his return to faith. It grieved him to realize he had used up so many of his years living out his own agenda. He honestly and sadly confessed,

"While I cannot make God the Lord of *all* my life, I can at least make him the Lord of what's left."

> WHILE WE CAN NEVER GIVE GOD ALL OUR YEARS, WE CAN HONESTLY GIVE HIM WHATEVER TIME WE HAVE LEFT.

Most of us face the same dilemma as my friend: we cannot give the entirety of our lives to God because we have already squandered too many of our years. Many people have already lived a significant portion of their lives before they come to faith in Christ. Others confess their sin at an early age but fall away later in life. But while we can never give God *all* our years, we can honestly give him the *remainder* of our lives.

My friend's phrase has become the watch-word of my life as well. Each morning I consciously quote Psalm 90:12. "Teach us to make the most of our time, so that we may grow in wisdom." I say to God, "I love you. I admire you. I consciously make you the God of what's left of my years." I cannot surrender the time I have lost, but I can let go of the time yet before me.

No matter what stage of life you are in, it is never too late to relinquish your time. One elderly believer I know who came to Christ late in life prayed, "God, there's not much of my life left, but all of it is yours. I give it freely. All I have left to give is my future."

I have a friend who was involved in a disastrous car wreck that should have taken his life. He crawled out of the crunched metal with barely a scratch. When he got back to his apartment that night, he was greeted by a poster he had earlier hung in his room. It was only a pop-art cliché, but it struck his

The Power of Letting Go

unsurrendered life with force. It read, "Today is the first day of the rest of your life!" He told me that as he read the words he was awakened to a fresh call from God. Life is precious—so precious it must be surrendered to God every morning, for each new morning is always the first day of the rest of our lives. Every sunrise is a chance to relinquish the coming day.

> PUSHING TO DO MORE "STUFF"— EVEN "CHRISTIAN STUFF"—IS NOT RELINQUISHMENT.

SABBATH REST

The counterpart to the problem of squandering our time is the problem of busyness. Just as we are called to let go of our time rather than hoard or waste it, we must also refrain from trying to pack too much into the time we have. God doesn't want us to chase after the clock. Christ is not flattered when we run madly about, trying to accomplish more than we have time for. Simply put,

I believe it is a sin to hassle our hurried schedules in the name of Jesus. To trade our neuroses for what we suppose to be God's neuroses is foolish indeed. Rushing to church is no evidence of a surrendered life. Pushing to do more "stuff"—even "Christian stuff"—is not relinquishment.

To be sure, God's perfect plan for his people involves work. Doing the work God has for us is part of living a life of obedience. But work ceases to be obedience when we are doing too much of it. For God's plan also involves rest. Rest is part of his desire for us. "Sabbath" is his gift to us. God's rest must bring to an end our chasing after the clock.

To relinquish our time is to welcome the cessation of all hurriedness—even Christian hurriedness. To let go of our schedules is to make our lives a Sabbath of peace wherein God replaces our tick-tocks and vibrations and ulcers with a practiced life of service.

"Sabbath" is what we gain when we let go

of schedules. *Sabbath* is the Hebrew number
seven, but it essentially symbolizes rest. The
Bible makes it clear that "rest" is the reward of
obedience: "To whom was God speaking
when he vowed that they would never enter
his place of rest? He was speaking to those
who disobeyed him. So we see that they were
not allowed to enter his rest because of their
unbelief" (Hebrews 3:18-19). We must let go
of hurriedness to take hold of health. We must
let go of time and take hold of his wonderful
peace. When our pointless panic is gone,
serenity becomes God's gift to us.

To let go of our mad whirl, we must
confess that we crave peace. We must admit
we are starved for time alone with him. We
must sing from our hearts:

"Sweet hour of prayer, sweet hour of
     prayer . . .
In seasons of distress and grief,
     My soul has often found relief.

And oft escaped the tempter's snare,
> By thy return, sweet hour of prayer."

Then comes the deliciousness of green
pastures and still waters. The world will lose
its hold on us when we face our appointment
books and tell them, "Get lost, I have an
appointment with my Lord! I want to treasure
every moment of my time with him."

Our days are not ours to fill up with activ-
ities of our choosing. Our time belongs to
God. We must not waste a moment! Remember, "A day is like a thousand years to the
Lord, and a thousand years is like a day"
(2 Peter 3:8).

TIME IS SHORT

I believe our lives have no point unless they
point to Christ. Without him, time has no
significance. If Jesus lives, the clock counts. If
Jesus does not live, the calendar is also dead.
But Jesus does live! And so I must surrender

all my hours to his glorification. I have a good role model for my abandonment. Jesus let go of every moment and gave everything to his Father. Every second of Christ's thirty-three years belonged to God. Not one moment of it was used to serve a selfish agenda. In the same way, we must relinquish every moment to Christ. He had no private agenda. Neither should we.

> WE MUST REMEMBER THAT TIME IS A LIMITED COMMODITY, AND WE ARE ALREADY RUNNING OUT OF IT!

Why is God so eager for us to surrender our time to him? Because he treasures our time with him. He desires our company! When in the Garden he said to his companions, "Couldn't you stay awake and watch with me even one hour?" (Matthew 26:40), he was saying to the apostles, "Could you not let go of the way you want to spend your time (in this case sleeping) and spend it the way I would like to have you spend it?"

Our time is ever to be his, and it means nothing while we hoard it for ourselves. We must remember that time is a limited commodity, and we are already running out of it! The message of Psalm 90:12 was summed up by a Celtic clockmaker who affixed this brass-plate phrase on the dial of each of his clocks:

> Lo, here I stand by thee upright
> > To give thee warning day and night.
> For every tick that I do give
> > Cuts short the time thou hast to live.

Jesus is coming to us, and we are going to him. We are ever working against this beautiful double deadline. We know not which of us shall be the first to reach the other. He could split the skies before we die! Or we could die before he comes. "The trumpet of the Lord shall sound and time shall be no more," says an old hymn, reminding us of the temporary nature of time.[8]

In the meantime, there is a mighty purpose in our minutes. We must never try to hoard the moments for ourselves. As T. S. Eliot put it, this futile attempt is but to measure out our lives in teaspoons. We are called to mightier living than this. We are to let go of time and gain eternity. We are to march into heaven singing the hymn of our daily surrender:

> Take my life and let it be
>> consecrated Lord to thee.
>> Take my moments and my days;
>> let them flow in ceaseless praise.[9]

✻ ✻ ✻ ✻

CHAPTER THREE

RELINQUISHING
OUR DREAMS

✳ ✳ ✳ ✳

*Alas! Every day we ask Him that His will may
be done; and when it comes to the doing, we have
such difficulty! We offer ourselves to God so
often; we say to Him at every step, "Lord, I am
yours, here is my heart;" and when He wants
to make use of us, we are so cowardly! How
can we say we are His, if we are unwilling
to accommodate our will to His?*

—ST. FRANCIS DE SALES[10]

✳ ✳ ✳ ✳

CALVIN MILLER

WRESTLING WITH GOD

Jacob was a man who, in spite of his weaknesses, was used mightily by God. This man, who deceived his own father in order to receive a blessing meant for his older brother, became the father of the twelve tribes of Israel. The story of Jacob gives me hope, for if God can use someone like Jacob, he can use anyone—even someone like me!

In Genesis 32:22-32 we find one of the most interesting and mysterious stories in the Bible. Jacob had been living in Haran, working for his father-in-law for the past twenty years. Now, at God's command, he was on his way back to Canaan with his family. When they came to the Jabbok River, Jacob sent everyone else across but remained behind by himself. During the night, we are told, "a man came and wrestled with him until dawn." Just before daybreak, the mysterious stranger "struck Jacob's hip and knocked it out of joint at the socket," leaving Jacob with a limp.

Before the man left, Jacob, still unsure of his adversary's identity, demanded a blessing from him. The man asked Jacob his name and then said, "Your name will no longer be Jacob. It is now Israel." At that moment Jacob knew the identity of the one with whom he had been wrestling. *Israel* means "one who struggles with God." Jacob had been wrestling all night with God himself!

WHEN WE LET GO OF OUR DREAMS, WE BEGIN TO LIVE LIVES THAT REALLY MATTER.

Throughout the Old Testament, we see the nation of Israel living up to the meaning of its name time and time again, as the Israelites continually struggled against the God who had chosen them as his own people. Today, believers struggle with the Almighty too! But our wrestling matches with our Creator don't need to set us against him.

I know many people who sometimes argue with God, yet they remain some of the happiest people I know. The effervescence of our faith should always keep us in the presence of God till we have wrangled through our needy moments. We may quarrel, but only as lovers. We must understand that there is nothing more wonderful than wrestling with God and losing the argument. For only when we cry "uncle" does God's better dream replace our own.

When we let go of our dreams, we begin to live lives that really matter. Many of God's servants have found themselves at Jabbok, Jacob's river of decision, wrestling with God. So will we. But at the end of our wrestling, God will have overcome us. We will have been wounded with a divine blow. And as we limp into the circle of light, all thought of doing our own will is laid aside. We are possessed by a new, infinitely better dream.

THE DESIRE TO HOLD ON

Part of our fondness for pursuing our own dreams rather than God's comes from the impression that our dreams might be easier to accomplish than his. One of my best, life-long friends is a man named Jim. Jim had a great deal of reluctance in coming to Christ. Once he arrived in the Lord's camp, he and God had the fiercest argument about his ability to do what God was asking him to do. God was calling him to be a preacher. Jim was convinced he would never be able to preach effectively. When Jim finally surrendered to God's dream, he was amazed to find that he was really very good at preaching. God was right! Only the initial idea was overwhelming.

Jim's struggle was much like that of the prophet Jeremiah.

Jeremiah knew the terrifying joy of God's call. When Jeremiah was a young man, God said to him, "I knew you before I formed you in your mother's womb. Before you were born I set you apart and appointed you as my spokesman to the world" (Jeremiah 1:5). There was no question in Jeremiah's mind

that God had an immense expectation of
him.

But Jeremiah wasn't ready to yield up his
own dreams for the ones God had for him just
yet. "O Sovereign Lord . . . I can't speak for
you!" he protested. "I'm too young!"

But his protest was fruitless! God touched
Jeremiah's mouth and said, "See, I have put
my words in your mouth" (Jeremiah 1:9).

And Jeremiah let go of his dreams. He
realized that it was far smarter to surrender his
own small, manageable dreams and latch on
to God's seemingly unmanageable will. And at
last he did; he ministered as God's prophet to
the nation of Judah for forty years. Jeremiah
let go of his own dreams and took hold of
history. Not a bad trade. But the wisdom of
the trade was only visible from the end of his
surrender and not from the moment he
decided to let go. No doubt he confessed the
glory of his relinquishment when later he
heard God's promise to his people: "I know

the plans I have for you. . . . They are plans for good and not for disaster, to give you a future and a hope" (Jeremiah 29:11).

The prophet Isaiah protested God's call by saying he was a "sinful man and a member of a sinful race" (Isaiah 6:5). Moses protested God's command to free his people from slavery in Egypt by saying that he was slow of speech and was really better suited to be a shepherd than a statesman-liberator (Exodus 4:10). It's not easy to follow God's call—but when we do, God brings about marvelous results.

> WE HAVE A FONDNESS FOR PURSUING OUR OWN DREAMS BECAUSE WE FEEL THAT OUR DREAMS MIGHT BE EASIER TO ACCOMPLISH THAN GOD'S.

I once planned to be a teacher—a science teacher. I was well into my university studies when the Soviets put up the first space satellite. It was called *Sputnik*, weighed 184 pounds, and orbited the world, burping forth only a beep. It was a mouse that roared. The rest of the world tuned into that mindless beep. The beep eventually thundered its way to becoming a Western inferiority complex. Free-world scientists stood in awe that the Soviets had beaten the Americans into space.

We felt better for a time when *Sputnik* fell out of the sky, disintegrating in its descent, after only months in orbit. But then the Soviets launched *Sputnik 2*—complete with a living dog, Laika. Americans were convinced that before we got our act together, our evil enemy would be raining down missiles from above!

When the Americans finally had a satellite ready for space, it was the size of a grapefruit and weighed less than four pounds. The *Vanguard* also beeped, but it was smaller than the soccer-ball-sized *Sputnik 1* and contained no dog like *Sputnik 2.* In comparison to the

Russian satellites, the American technological effort seemed small and shameful.

These beepers following their mindless orbits changed history. The outcome of their output was an outcry. Americans lamented loudly that we had fallen behind the Russians and needed thousands more young people to enter into education and science. I was at that very time majoring in physics and chemistry, and so—in my own mind—was sitting pretty. Like these primitive satellites, the salaries for science teachers went into orbit. I was wonderfully enthusiastic and ready to begin my life as a science teacher.

God, however, was less excited about my plans. God felt that I should be a preacher! "Do you know what preachers make in a year?" I asked God. He knew.

"Don't you know that a lot of preachers are 'spacey?' And no preacher has ever put anything into orbit!" He knew that, too.

But the worst problem was that the whole

idea terrorized me. I explained to God that my current pastor—the only person I really knew who said he had been called to preach—was balding, overweight, and not a good role model for sermon delivery. In fact, my pastor's insistence that he had been called to preach by God made God look like a poor career counselor. But God assured me that even though my preacher was less than a riveting speaker, that didn't change my own calling.

When I told my sister that God had called me to preach, she was sure that God had gotten a wrong number and that once God heard me, he would forget the whole thing. I was in agony. But I was out of arguments. God was calling me to preach, and there was nothing I could do or say to convince him to change his mind.

Accepting my call turned into one long, horrible march through my hell of unwilling surrender. Why couldn't God have called me to be a science teacher, like I wanted? That would be a much simpler, far less challenging life plan. I didn't really mind relinquishing my teaching dreams; they didn't seem all that noble, even to me. But I froze at the thought of preaching the Word of God.

I finally decided I would prove my point to God. In two very short sermons I was able to prove how inept I was. I'm sure he agreed with the audiences where I preached that these first efforts were poor. But God, who knew the end from the beginning, could see what was invisible to the audiences. He knew my preaching would, with time, improve. So I let go!

> ONLY WHEN WE LET GO OF OUR LITTLE CAN WE TAKE HOLD OF GOD'S MUCH.

But my yielding was done with great pain. Over the years, I think I have improved at the art of preaching, but it is still the hardest work I know. I ever struggle to preach well, yet so often I feel my sermons have failed to meet the high standard I know God has set for me. I have written a couple of thousand sermons over my lifetime and have even produced text-books on the subject. But still I sometimes feel that I have not preached in a way that does credit to my Father in heaven.

Yet despite my occasional feelings of inadequacy, God has used me. He has helped me plant a flourishing church that has grown to a membership of several thousand. He has led me throughout much of the world, teaching and evangelizing. The message of my life is unmistakable: Relinquishing my own easy dreams and following God's difficult one was the right course.

Once when I was pastor of a little church, I fell in love with the loveliest member of the congregation. When we finally began to date, I told her that God had called me to preach and that, while I loved her, I wouldn't ask her to marry me unless she felt called to live with a man who had this calling. Bit by bit she relinquished the private dreams she had, and together we embarked on a rich adventure. My wife and I have now walked this path together for forty-five years. By God's grace we have seen thousands of people come to faith in Christ, and we have seen several millions of copies of my books printed in many languages and distributed around the world. The wonderful decades of our life are a testimony that yielding is the key. Only when we let go of our little can we take hold of God's much.

✷ ✷ ✷ ✷

CHAPTER FOUR

RELINQUISHING OUR SELF-IMAGE

✳ ✳ ✳ ✳

*Answering the call of our Creator is "the ultimate
why" for living, the highest source of purpose in
human existence. Apart from such a calling, all
hope of discovering purpose (as in the current talk
of shifting "from success to significance") will end
in disappointment. To be sure, calling is not what
it is commonly thought to be. It has to be dug out
from under the rubble of ignorance and confusion.
And, uncomfortably, it often flies directly in the
face of our human inclinations. But nothing short
of God's call can ground and fulfill the truest
human desire for purpose.*

—OS GUINNESS[11]

✳ ✳ ✳ ✳

NAGGING DOUBT

Perhaps the last thing we ever let go of is our pride. We work hard to hold on to our image. The way we appear to ourselves and others is important to us, and we want to be sure that we project well in our communities, workplaces, and even churches. We shudder to think how we would feel if people could suddenly become aware of all the things we hide from them to keep our reputation intact.

Who are you really? How can you be sure that you are being seen exactly as you want others to see you? Such questions tend to lead to self-doubt, and self-doubt is the first and most powerful ingredient of low self-esteem, an affliction nearly everyone faces. Most of us suffer from a limited self-image. We are shot through with inferiority. I once heard a joke with the punch line, "Never worry too much about low self-esteem, it is common to all losers." Many of us believe it.

But rest assured, God is not the sponsor of

our low self-esteem. In fact, God went to great lengths to keep us from thinking poorly of ourselves. Would you be willing to die for someone you thought was worthless? Of course not, and neither would God. Jesus' death on the cross was the ultimate expression of his incredible love for us, a love that gives us incredible worth. We were created in God's image (Genesis 1:27). When we fail to love ourselves, we insult God's creativity and sin against the passion of God's grace.

> GOD WENT TO GREAT LENGTHS TO KEEP US FROM THINKING POORLY OF OURSELVES.

There is an exercise I like to encourage people to try. From time to time as you continue your pilgrimage through life, write down your name on a piece of paper. Then study it for a while. If you can, find out what your name means. Pray over it. After a while, you'll begin to see your name as a covenant of celebration. It identifies you as a person, someone who is unique and special. In moments of despondency, never forget that whatever your name is, it is important to God.

THE INFERIORITY MALAISE

All of my life I have suffered from feelings of inferiority. It took me a long time to come to grips with the idea that I was strategically important to God. Even after I became a believer, it took me years to acknowledge that my self-definition was of some consequence to God.

The fact is that you and I do matter to God. We matter not because of who we are but because we are the prized possessions of a God who spent himself to buy our souls. Still, we often bumble through life riddled with feelings of inferiority.

Remember Jeremiah? When God called the young man to preach, he balked, offering as his argument his repugnant feelings of inferiority. "I can't do it," he cried. "I'm afraid. I'm not adequate. If somehow conditions were better or I were in the right place . . . if only I had more confidence, I'd try it. But as I am now, it's not possible." But God raised Jeremiah up from the strangling mishmash of his inferiority.

> TOO MANY CHRISTIANS ARE PSYCHOLOGICAL DISASTER CASES CRYING OUT THEIR POOR SELF-IMAGE BEFORE A GOD WHO SEES ONLY THEIR GLORY.

I have seen many modern-day Jeremiahs in my years of ministry. So many of us are psychological disaster cases crying out our poor self-image before a God who sees only our glory. But this glory never occurs to us when we go around feeling bad about who we are rather than accepting God's evaluation of us.

A cartoon I recently saw in a book pictured a psychiatrist sending his receptionist out into his crowded waiting room. The doctor says to her, "Send the paranoids in first—the ones with inferiority complexes don't mind waiting."

The cartoon is not altogether true. People with inferiority complexes *do* mind. But because they are so deluded by weak self-image, the only solution they can find to their problems is to whine before God that they somehow deserve a better self-image than they have. Although they live constantly within the affirming love of God, they mock it with their own dour mood. Eventually, they develop an emotional dependence on their inferiority; they only feel good when they feel really bad.

To some, such people may appear modest, but in reality they are simply "whipped." They love to sing, "Oh, to be nothing, nothing!" But they hardly sing it out of healthy humility. In fact, they'd rather be singing, "Oh, to be something, something!" But they feel they're not worthy. I have met people who were so down on themselves that I thought their telephone answering machines must say something like, "I'm sorry, so very terribly, horribly sorry I can't come to the phone right now. I doubt if you have an important message to leave me—I mean, who would? But if you do, leave it after the tone. Have a nice day, and remember that God loves a suffering spirit."

> GOD CALLS US TO LET GO OF OUR POOR SELF-IMAGE AND GRAB ON TO HIS VIEW OF US.

Inferiority is a common malaise among Christians. I have seen believers with incredible vision lose their dream of God because they were swamped by feelings of self-pity and inability. One such person was Fred Z. Fred and I wound up as church planters in the same city. It was hard work, and both of us were often beset by feelings of low achievement and a zero self-image. After a series of events in which Fred lost his church, he spent a great many months in a hospital, lost in despair. Why? He never learned that God can renovate the yielded heart, cleansing our low self-esteem and gilding our inadequacies with power. I take no credit for achieving what Fred did not. All I did was set my inferiority complex before a renovating God who convinced me that he could turn my drab incapacity into great achievement.

GRABBING ON TO SIGNIFICANCE

God calls us to let go of our poor self-image and grab on to his view of us. He calls us to make a healthy new covenant with ourselves to see ourselves through his eyes. Do you ever hear yourself lamenting the smallness of your role in the sizable Christian pageant that we call the kingdom of God? Take heart. Jesus came to magnify your importance, not reduce it. He specifically called you, a specific individual, to a specific assignment. *"You are special!*" he says to you. What right do you have to stand against God's view of you? What right do you have to diminish heaven's esteem? What right to you have to stand back and negate your special place in God's kingdom?

IT'S NOT EASY TO LET GO . . . BUT WHEN YOU DO, YOU WILL FIND THAT YOU HAVE LOST NOTHING AND GAINED EVERYTHING.

It is unnecessary for you to stand and cry, "Oh, to be nothing, nothing." Such self-deprecation is redundant. There will likely be many flippant foes throughout your life who will be saying that of you. Don't add to the mayhem with your own voice of self-doubt!

But if you insist on thinking that you are "nothing, nothing," please give up the folly of doing it on God's time. He has a big lost world to redeem and is counting on your significance, not your nothingness, to get it done.

Inferiority always comes because we measure who we are or where we are against those who seem to be more and have more than we do. The truth is, God doesn't care about such things. God loves people right where he finds them. And willingness, not skill, is the key to his use. You've probably heard the cliché, "God wants our availability, not our ability." It's true.

God said to Jeremiah, "Before I formed you, I knew you! Before I formed you, I called you to be something brand new." With divine fingers God shapes every person in the womb into an image and form like his own. Each precisely etched embryo is a person whom God has laid out for his own use from eternity past. Each one of us has been known and loved since the beginning of time—even before the world was made! To have been loved an eternity before our arrival is a great reason for getting rid of our feelings of inferiority.

Consider the words of Psalm 139:13-16:

You made all the delicate, inner parts of
my body
and knit me together in my mother's
womb.
Thank you for making me so wonderfully
complex!
Your workmanship is marvelous—and
how well I know it.
You watched me as I was being formed in
utter seclusion,
as I was woven together in the dark of
the womb.
You saw me before I was born.
Every day of my life was recorded in
your book.
Every moment was laid out
before a single day had passed.

God called us to significance even before
he placed us in the womb. How could we
think that God could ever be haphazard in his

plans for our lives? There is no need ever to be confused about who we are or what we mean to God. His Word is clear: God created us, and he loves us. God made each individual unique. We are created in God's own image.

If you are tempted to hold on to feelings of inferiority, it is not God who is whispering messages of inadequacy to your heart; it is your own sinful nature. Such messages are poisonous darts shot by the enemy to destroy who you are and what you mean. They are an affront to the Divine, a blatant denial of God's love. Don't listen! Don't give in to the temptation to wallow in your weakness!

It's not easy to let go of your self-image, just as it's not easy to let go of your striving for material possessions, your time, or your dreams. But letting go is vital to your walk with a God who loves you more than you could possibly imagine. When you let go, you will find that you have lost nothing and gained everything.

Let go!

Relinquish!

Cast off your weakness.

Lay hold of his strength.

The rags of your pretense are leprous with infection.

Clothe yourself with his impenetrable armor of life.

God is your defense! Your peace!

You are here by divine appointment.

God loves you! You are important to him!

Get on your knees, let go of your weakness, and don't get off your knees until you're ready to accept your place in God's strategic plan.

✳ ✳ ✳ ✳

CONCLUSION

God has implanted in your heart his wisdom. So throw out of your heart everything that contradicts this wisdom

—HILDEGARD OF BINGEN[12]

The city of Rome is built on a bed of soft volcanic rock, through which run miles of lava tunnels. In ancient times, the first Christians used these vast underground passageways as burial grounds for the thousands upon thousands of martyrs who died for Christ in the Roman arenas. Today the word used to describe these underground cemeteries is *catacombs*.

One of the most famous catacombs in Rome is the Catacombs of Saint Sebastian. I once visited those dark, dank passageways and learned that the bodies of the apostles Peter and Paul are thought to have been temporarily buried there to protect them during the first barbarian invasions of Rome. I saw one spot on one of those walls where a piece of plate glass protected a very ancient etching. The names of Peter and Paul are recorded there, scratched in the stone by some ancient hand: *Paule et Petre petite pro Victore.*

Who can ever be sure if the words are really authentic? They might have been put there by Indiana Jones or a tourist from Peoria. But, on the other hand, they might actually have been put there by a first-century Christian burying a martyred loved one.

The prayer will not leave me—*Paul and Peter, pray for us. Pray for our martyrs.* It sticks in my heart. I think of the hundreds of early Christians who once visited those sunless tubes, trying to figure out who they were and how they were going to answer their world in a desperate time.

> YOUR FINGERS WERE NOT MADE TO GRASP; THEY WERE JOINTED IN SPINDLING KNUCKLES TO ALLOW YOU THE JOY OF LETTING GO.

But I believe those who were martyred did not die in confusion. They knew who they were! They knew that there was power for the living and grace for the dying in one simple word: *Relinquish!* And so they did. They let go of their dreams, their priorities, and even their lives—and the world reeled under the powerful impact of Jesus.

We are the born-again lovers of God. When we confessed our sin and accepted Christ's life-giving sacrifice, we traversed the birth canal to become significant.

But how are we to grow and mature in this significance?

It is simple, but it requires all the courage you have.

Let go of the little; take hold of the much.

Relinquish your folly, and garner God's wisdom.

Your fingers were not made to grasp; they were jointed in spindling knuckles to allow you the joy of letting go.

So, hold on no longer.

When your hands are free of self, you will find your arms are wings, to let you fly forever in the counsel of Christ's obedience. You were meant to live in heaven. Let go of earth.

NOTES

[1] Tricia McCary Rhodes, *Taking Up Your Cross* (Minneapolis, MN: Bethany House Publishers, 2000), 57.

[2] Hazel Felleman, ed., *Poems That Live Forever* (New York: Doubleday, 1965), 337.

[3] F. B. Meyer, *Our Daily Homily* (London: Marshall Morgan & Scott, 1951), 73.

[4] Saint Alphonsus Maria De Liguori, *The Life of Sorrow Which Jesus Led from His Birth* taken from *Book of Novenas* in Calvin Miller, *The Book of Jesus* (NY: Simon & Schuster, 1996), 249.

[5] Saint Alphonsus Maria De Liguori, *The Life of Sorrow Which Jesus Led from His Birth* taken from *Book of Novenas* in Calvin Miller, *The Book of Jesus* (NY: Simon & Schuster, 1996), 249.

[6] Henry Barraclough, *Ivory Palaces,* in *Songs of Faith and Praise* (West Monroe, LA: Howard Publishers, 1994), no. 896.

[7] Thomas à Kempis, *Come, Lord Jesus,* ed. David Hazard (Minneapolis, MN: Bethany House Publishers, 1999), 89.

[8] James M. Black, *When the Roll Is Called up Yonder,* in *Worship His Majesty* (Alexandria, IN: Gaither Music Co., 1987), no. 692.

[9] Francis R. Havergal, *Take My Life and Let It Be,* in *Worship His Majesty* (Alexandria, IN: Gaither Music Co., 1987), no. 380.

[10] St. Francis de Sales, *Thy Will Be Done* (Manchester, NH: Sophia Institute Press, 1995), 8.

[11] Os Guinness, *The Call* (Nashville, TN: Word Publishing, 1998), 4.

[12] Robert Van de Weyer, ed., *Hildegard in a Nutshell* (London: Hodder & Stoughton, 1997), 19.